LIVES
AND
TIMES

St Francis

Penelope Harnett

Heinemann
LIBRARY

First published in Great Britain by Heinemann Library
Halley Court, Jordan Hill, Oxford OX2 8EJ,
a division of Reed Educational and Professional Publishing Ltd.

OXFORD FLORENCE PRAGUE MADRID ATHENS
MELBOURNE AUCKLAND KUALA LUMPUR SINGAPORE TOKYO
IBADAN NAIROBI KAMPALA JOHANNESBURG GABORONE
PORTSMOUTH NH (USA) CHICAGO MEXICO CITY SAO PAULO

Designed by Ken Vail Graphic Design, Cambridge
Illustrations by Jon Davies (Linden Artists)
Printed and bound in Italy by L.E.G.O.

01 00 99 98 97
10 9 8 7 6 5 4 3 2 1

ISBN 0 431 02476 6

Some words are shown in bold, **like this**.
You can find out what they mean by
looking in the glossary. The glossary also
helps you say difficult words.

British Library Cataloguing in Publication Data

Harnett, Penelope
St Francis - (Lives & times)
1. Francis, of Assisi, Saint, 1182–1226 - Juvenile literature
2. Christian saints - Italy - Biography - Juvenile literature
I. Title
270'.092

Acknowledgements
The Publishers would like to thank the following for permission to reproduce photographs:
Archiv Fur Kunst und Geschichte, p.18; Bridgeman Art Library, p.19; Heseltine, John, p.23; Scala, pp.17,
20, 21, 22.

Cover photograph: Scala

Our thanks to Betty Root for her comments in the preparation of this book.

Every effort has been made to contact copyright holders of any material reproduced in this book. Any
omissions will be rectified in subsequent printings if notice is given to the Publisher.

Contents

The first part of this book tells you the story of St Francis.
The second part tells you how we can find out about his life.

Childhood

In 1181, over 800 years ago, a baby boy was born in Italy, in a town called **Assisi**. His name was Francis. This is a story about his life.

Francis's father was a very rich
merchant. Francis helped him to buy
and sell rolls of cloth.

Growing up

Francis had lots of friends. He liked wearing fine clothes and going to parties. But Francis was not always happy.

One day Francis went into a church. He heard a voice speaking to him. 'Go and repair my church,' said the voice. Francis thought it was God's voice.

A terrible quarrel

Soon after, Francis stole some cloth from his father and sold it to help repair the church. His father was very angry. 'Give me the money,' he said. 'It belongs to me.'

'You can have everything which belongs to you,' said Francis. He took off all his fine clothes and gave them to his father.
A man heard the quarrel and put his cloak over Francis.

Repairing the church

Francis left home. He had no money and he had to beg for food. He began to repair the church in **Assisi** with his own hands.

Now Francis was happy. He talked to people about God and the wonderful world which he believed God had made.

The wolf

Francis made friends with animals and birds. He was very kind to people, too. Once he visited a town where everybody was afraid of a fierce wolf. Francis went to meet the wolf.

'Tell the people you are sorry, and that you will not frighten them anymore,' said Francis. Everybody in the town watched as the wolf held up its paw to shake Francis's hand.

Rules

Many people wanted to live like Francis.
Francis told them to give everything away
and to help poor and sick people. He
taught them to **pray** and to be kind to all
living things.

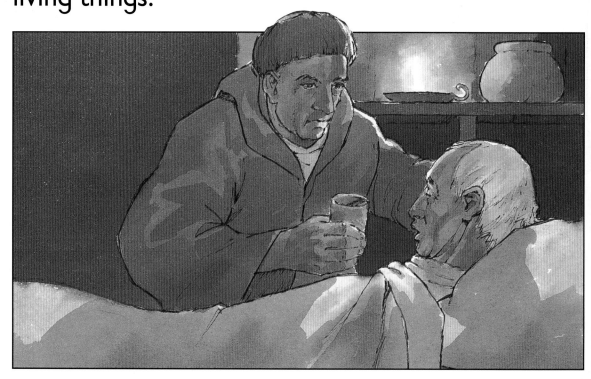

Francis wrote a list of rules about how to
live a good life and help other people. Men
who followed these rules were called **friars**.

Francis dies

Francis became ill. There is a story that as Francis lay dying, a flock of skylarks flew up into the sky. They sang sweetly as he died.

The church of St Francis

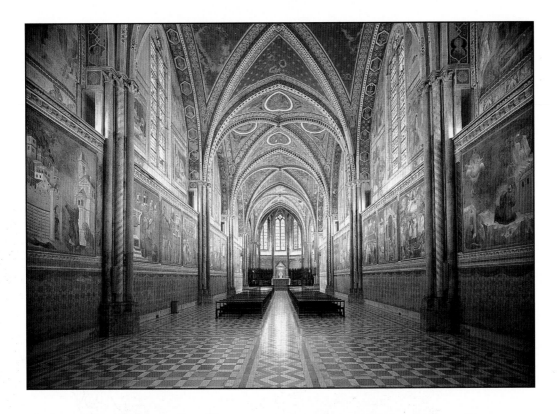

After his death, Francis was made a **saint**. A beautiful church was built in the town of **Assisi** to remember him by. It is still there, and this photograph shows how it looks now.

Stories and pictures

We know about St Francis's life from the stories of **friars**. Friars travelled around the world telling people stories about Francis. His life and his rules were not forgotten. These men are friars.

Artists painted pictures on church walls.
These pictures are called **frescoes**. They
too tell the story of St Francis. They show
many of the things Francis did. You can
still see them in **Assisi** today.

Buildings and museums

In Italy, people visit the churches and quiet places where Francis **prayed.** Some pray near the cave and woods where Francis often stayed.

Francis told his **friars** they should not have many clothes. Francis's tunic is now in a **museum**. You can see that it was very plain.

Letters and teachings

Francis wrote letters to **friars**. This one, to Friar Leo, can still be seen today. In it Francis asked God to look after Friar Leo.

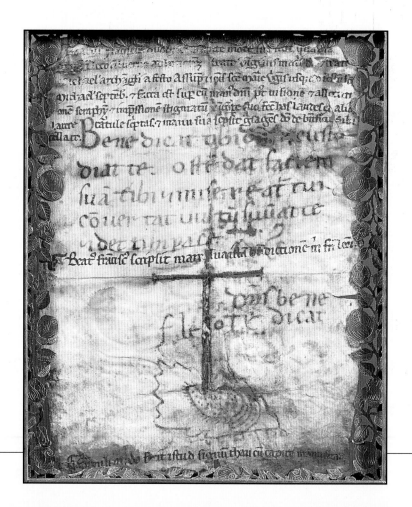

Friars still follow Francis's rules today.
They work in churches, schools, hospitals,
prisons and wherever people need help.

Glossary

This glossary explains difficult words, and helps you to say words which are hard to say.

Assisi a town in Italy. You say *a-SEE-see*

friar man who follows St Francis's rules. You say *fry-er*

frescoes wall paintings, often on church walls. You say *FRESS-kose*

merchant person who buys and sells

museum place to see old and interesting things. You say *mew-ZI-em*

pray talk to God

saint people who lived a very good life and were very close to God when they were alive

Index